An Italian Pantry

Olive

Leonardo Romanelli
Gabriella Ganugi

An Italian Pantry

Oil

WINE APPRECIATION GUILD

Also available in
"An Italian Pantry":

CHEESE

PASTA

PROSCIUTTO

First Published in North America 2004
The Wine Appreciation Guild
360 Swift Avenue
South San Francisco CA 94080

ISBN 1-891267-55-8

This book was conceived, edited and designed by
McRae Books Srl, Florence, Italy.

Project Manager: Anne McRae
Text: Gabriella Ganugi and Leonardo Romanelli
Photography: Marco Lanza, Walter Mericchi
Set Design: Rosalba Gioffrè
Design: Marco Nardi
Editing: Anne McRae, Holly Willis

2 4 6 8 10 9 7 5 3 1

Color separations: Fotolito Toscana, Florence, Italy
Printed and bound in China

Contents

Introduction

Olive oil is an ancient food, born in the Mediterranean and as central to its cuisines and cultures as bread. Properly produced extra-virgin olive oil is one of the purest and healthiest fats available. It is a versatile fat too, and can be used with equal success to sauté, bake, roast, or fry a wide range of foods. In some parts of Italy, it even replaces butter in recipes for cakes and cookies. But the best olive oils only come into their own when served raw, over a simple *bruschetta* (slice of toasted bread, rubbed with garlic, and dusted with a little salt and pepper), a fresh green salad, or a slice of Pecorino cheese.

Olive oil is unique because it combines the pleasures of the palate with the virtues of healthy eating. Thanks to its high oleic acid content, extra-virgin olive oil protects the heart and arteries, slowing down the aging process. It lowers low-density lipoprotein cholesterol levels ("bad" cholesterol) and raises high-density lipoprotein levels ("good" cholesterol). Olive oil is easy to digest, whether raw or cooked, because of its high composition of fatty acids. Rich in vitamins A, D, and E, it is the perfect aid for the body's natural defenses against digestive sicknesses, aging of the bones, and arteriosclerosis. Extra-virgin olive oil is also a mild laxative; a tablespoon a day in the morning on an empty stomach acts against constipation. Externally, it can be used for massaging joints stiff with arthritis. In ancient times, it was massaged on the temples against headache and migraines and in the mouth for weak gums.

Today, olive oil is internationally recognized as one of the healthiest fats. But its therapeutic qualities were already well-known and described by the Greek doctor Galeno, in the 2nd century AD.

A fresh bowl of mixed salad greens makes an eyecatching starter or side dish. To dress, sprinkle with a little salt and pepper, drizzle with a dash of vinegar or freshly squeezed lemon juice, and then drizzle with extra-virgin olive oil (the oil should always be the last ingredient because it coats the greens). Toss and serve.

Olive oil is also excellent for cooking. Even at high heats, when frying, for instance, it is less likely to decompose because it reaches "smoking point" (when fats become dangerous) at a much higher temperature than any other oil. When served raw to dress salads and other foods, it can be used in smaller quantities than many oils because of its strong aromatic flavors. Thus, even though it is a high calorie food, it can be used sparingly with excellent results. These and its many other health-giving properties have made olive oil popular around the world.

Late November, when the new season's Tuscan oils begin to appear in the stores and markets, is the ideal time to serve fettunta *(the Tuscan word for* bruschetta*). The peppery oil and the bite of the garlic, mellows out on the unsalted Tuscan bread for a taste explosion.*

Italy ranks second in olive oil production after Spain, although in terms of quality, Italian extra-virgin oils are still the most highly prized and sought after. As the use of olive oil has spread, people have become more knowledgeable and discriminating in their choice of oils. Nowadays, in good restaurants the world over, you may well be presented with a list of oils along with the wine list. This book will give you a good introduction to oils from all the oil-producing regions of Italy. It will tell you how to choose them, how to match them to the food you are preparing, how to store them, how to fry with them, plus a host of other suggestions for their use, as well as anecdotes on production and history.

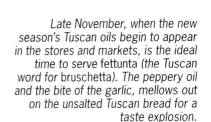

The Story of Olive Oil

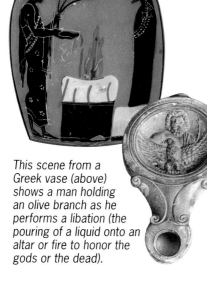

This scene from a Greek vase (above) shows a man holding an olive branch as he performs a libation (the pouring of a liquid onto an altar or fire to honor the gods or the dead).

This ancient Greek vase (below) shows farmers harvesting the olives by shaking them out of the trees using long sticks (a method still used today). The Greeks gave pride of place to the olive in their culture. One famous myth tells how Zeus decided to award the city of Athens to the god or goddess who created the most useful gift. Athena made the olive tree and won the competition.

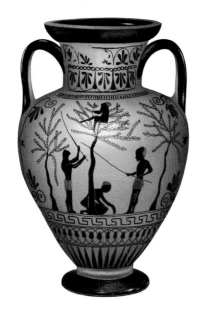

The olive tree comes originally from the lands of the Eastern Mediterranean, where it was probably one of the earliest plants to be cultivated. Records show that olives were being grown on the island of Crete by 3,500 BC. In ancient times the olive was considered sacred by all the Mediterranean peoples, and its oil was used in religious ceremonies and rituals. The Egyptians considered it a gift from the gods, the Phoenicians called it "liquid gold," and the Hebrews used it to anoint their kings.

The Greeks brought the olive tree to Italy, where the Etruscans were the first to use it for cooking. Before then it was used for medicinal purposes, as a cosmetic, in perfume making, or as a fuel to be burned in lamps. The Romans consumed vast quantities of olive oil and many of their finest writers took time to explain how to make it, as well as extolling its many virtues. Columella, in his 1st century AD treatise *De Re Rustica* called the olive "the first among all plants." As the Romans conquered the Mediterranean, they divided their new provinces into oil-making regions. Rome itself was the center of the massive oil trade, and prices, trade routes, and supplies were controlled from the *Arca Olearia*, a financial market in the capital.

With the fall of the Roman Empire and the centuries of decline that followed, the cultivation of olives became too time consuming for the shifting populations. The production of olive oil was kept alive in Christian monasteries where the monks used it in their religious rites. As the economy recovered after 1100, olive farming became widespread again in Italy. During the later Middle Ages southern Italy, especially Apulia, was transformed into a gigantic olive grove. The merchants of the wealthy city-states in central and northern Italy, such as Venice, Florence, and Genoa, exported Italian oil east to Byzantium and Egypt and north to the cities of Europe.

Olive farming and the commerce of oil continued through the 16th and 17th centuries, dimmed occasionally by poor harvests or bad markets. In the 18th century, olive tree varieties were for the first time classified according to their geographic origins. Italian olive oil gained an international reputation for its quality and taste. The powerful merchants of Venice created a consortium, called the *Negozio di Ponente,* to export Italian products, (including olive oil) to the flourishing cities of northern Europe. During that century, Tuscany and Apulia earned the reputation of producing the best olive oil and of having the most extensive olive groves. Olive growing increased in Liguria too, as farmers began to cultivate olives on their own, without mixing them in among other plants. In the 19th century Umbria also became an important supplier.

In the late 19th and early 20th centuries olive oil suffered a "dark age" of sorts. The great changes brought about by the industrial revolution in the 19th century and the two world wars of the 20th century, during which olive trees were burned when all the coal was used in the war effort, led to changes in eating habits. A return to animal fats and seed oils caused a decline in the production of olive oil. However, the final decades of the 20th century brought a new boom, as the benefits of the traditional Mediterranean diet were rediscovered. Today, Italy is a world leader in the production and export of quality extra-virgin oils.

There are many references to the olive in the Bible. In the story of the great flood, it is only when the dove returns with an olive branch that Noah is convinced that the waters are receding. The olive and its precious oil have retained an important role in Christian symbolism (as a peace offering, for example) and rites. In the Roman Catholic Church olive oil is present in many ceremonies in a believer's life, from birth (with baptism) to death (with the Last Rites).

9

This Renaissance dish by Italian artist Luca Della Robbia is one of a series showing the various typical occupations for each month. November is for picking olives.

Making Olive Oil

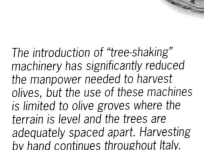

Harvesting the olives for the new season's oil is a delicate operation. To ensure quality, both timing and method are of fundamental importance. Olives mature in late fall. The best time to harvest them is as they are just turning from green to black when they contain the most oil of the best quality. However, the olives don't all mature at the same time, even on the same tree. Except on very small, family-run olive farms, it is not economically advantageous to pick the olives from each tree several times, so farmers need to chose the time when the largest possible number of olives are mature. In the past, it was widely believed that waiting for all the olives to mature would produce a better oil and this caused the harvest to be put off, sometimes until early spring. This led to the production of overly sweet oils with very high acid levels.

Only fresh olives still attached to the tree can be made into high quality oil or processed for the table, so they must be detached from the plant not picked up from the ground. The harvesting technique depends on the type of tree as well as the lie of the land. The simplest technique is the manual *brucatura*. This is the slowest method and involves the picking of ripe olives only and must be repeated several times during the fall, winter, and sometimes even into the spring. The *pettinatura* method involves the use of a special hand-held rake. Its use is limited to small olive trees where the top branches are still within arm's reach. Taller trees are harvested using the *bacchiatura* method which involves beating the branches with poles and catching the olives on sheets of canvas spread on the ground under the tree.

10

The introduction of "tree-shaking" machinery has significantly reduced the manpower needed to harvest olives, but the use of these machines is limited to olive groves where the terrain is level and the trees are adequately spaced apart. Harvesting by hand continues throughout Italy.

Botanically, the olive is classed as a drupe, along with peaches and plums. The olive tree (Olea europaea) is an evergreen, ranging in height from 10 to 40 feet (3 to 12 meters) and more. Its leaves are dark green on top and a beautiful silver color underneath. Olive trees bloom in late spring. There are two types of flowers: perfect, with both male and female parts, which develop into fruit; and male, which contain only pollen-producing parts. Pollination takes place by wind and the olives reach maturity 6 to 8 months after the blossoms appear.

Many producers claim that mechanical harvest leads to poorer quality oils, others say that there really is no difference.

Opinions vary about whether hand picked olives are of higher quality than those harvested mechanically. The high cost of manual harvesting (about 50 percent of the cost involved in the production of oil can be attributed to the harvest), has meant that the transition to mechanical harvesting has been made wherever possible. However, many areas where olives are grown, such as steep hill country, especially when terraced, and other areas of rough or wasteland, are unsuitable for machinery. Manual harvesting continues in these areas. Overall, the high cost of harvesting is gradually increasing the quality of the end product, since it can only be paid for by producing better oils.

During the first step in the production of olive oil, made according to the traditional method, the olives are crushed by a large granite wheel.

As the olives are harvested they are mounded up into heaps in large containers where, like all plant matter, they begin to heat up and ferment. This can damage the quality of the end product because the heat and humidity develop into molds which contaminate the flavor of the oil. For this reason the olives must be moved to the press as quickly as possible. To ensure quality, the olives must be pressed within 36 hours of harvesting.

The harvest season is concentrated in just a few short weeks and during that time everyone wants their olives pressed as soon as possible. The few mills available work under extreme pressure. In recent years a number of large, fast mills have been installed as well as many smaller, cheaper mills, so that olives picked during the day can be processed that same evening. As the demand for both the quantity and quality of Italian oils increases it seems likely that more and more of these mills will be built.

Stacking the disks containing the mats through which the oil will drain during pressing.

The transition from olive to olive oil comes about through the following processes: *frangitura* (crushing), *gramolatura* (pressing), and the *estrazione* (extraction).

Before crushing, any leaves and twigs are removed and the olives are washed and dried. They are then crushed, either using the traditional huge stone wheels (left) or stainless steel hammers, into a paste containing both the olive pulp and the pits. The paste is then spread on hemp or nylon mats which are placed in metal disks. The disks are stacked up in batches of 30 or 40 on a hydraulic press and are then pressed so that a reddish brown liquid composed of oil and water drips out through the porous mats and accumulates in the bottom of the press. From there it is drained off into a separator where the water and oil are separated in a centrifuge. The oil is then drained out into tanks where it is stored until ready for bottling or canning for sales.

The olive solids and the water are usually gathered up and sent to a refinery where their last drops of oil are extracted. The resulting oil is used to fertilize the land, as cattle food, or put to industrial use. This is the traditional method of making oil. Some modern mills bypass some of these steps or combine them all in a continual mechanical process. The oils produced by modern mechanical means can be just as good as those made according to the traditional method.

TYPES OF OLIVE OIL

The quality of olive oils is measured not only in terms of taste but also according to levels of acidity. The lower the level of acidity, the better the quality of the oil. Levels of acidity and the labels that oils are allowed to carry are controlled in Italy by strict EC regulations.

Olio Extravergine di Oliva (Extra-virgin olive oil): this is the top quality olive oil. To qualify for this label olive oil must be produced in a cold press (i.e. no heat must be applied during the extraction of the oil); must have an acidity level lower than 1 percent; and must also have excellent color, aroma, and flavor.

Olio Vergine di Oliva (Virgin olive oil): this oil must have an acidity level below 2 percent and must also have very good color, aroma, and flavor.

Olio di Oliva Vergine Corrente (Plain olive oil): this label is for oils in which acidity does not exceed 3.3 percent. They must also have good color, aroma, and flavor.

Oils with higher levels of acidity or with defects in color, aroma, and flavor are known in Italy as *olio lampante* (which literally means "shining oil," perhaps because it was used in oil lamps). They must be further refined before they can be sold as olive oil.

Top: olive paste.
Above: the new oil trickles out of the centrifuge.

Below: new Tuscan oil is often a lovely bright green.

Appreciating Olive Oil

Italian olive oils exhibit every style and flavor, from sweet and fruity with very little bite, through to strong and peppery with pungent aftertastes. They also come in a range of colors, from deep, dark green to pale, golden yellow. Despite what you may have heard, there is no one "correct" color, nor even a "right" aroma and flavor. It is really a matter of personal preference, and food combining. You wouldn't use a strong, peppery oil on a delicate dish, such as boiled fish, because it would overpower the fish instead of enhancing its refined flavors.

The color of olive oil is defined mainly by liposoluble pigments such as xantophyl, chlorophyll, carotene, and carotenoids. If the chlorophyll predominates, the oil will have a bright green color, whereas if the carotene and carotenoids are more abundant, the oil will appear more golden yellow in color.

Olive oil needs to be stored away from bright light to stop it from spoiling. Traditional containers were made of pottery or shaded glass.

The flavor is due not only to the ripeness of the olives when harvested, but also to the method of extraction used, and to environmental factors. The mild climate of certain regions for example, allows for the olives to be harvested throughout the winter until late spring, and produces an oil which is both sweet and full-bodied. Many freshly pressed olive oils tend to have a bitter and almost spicy flavor due to the fact that the olives were under-ripe when pressed.

When the new oils appear in Italy starting from late fall, prospective buyers are enticed by the offer of tiny squares of bread to dip into the *olio nuovo*. If you get the chance, do taste your olive oil before buying it. Smell is very important in determining the quality and style of an oil, as well as its age. We have sometimes seen exported oils on sale far from their Mediterranean homes that would make their makers turn pale. Olive oil doesn't keep for very long and it can easily become rancid if stored unwisely. If it smells dicey, put it back on the shelf. Sniffing the oil's aroma will also tell you a lot about its character. As you proceed to taste the oil, decide what you are looking for and what you like

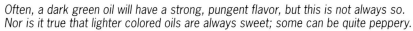

Calabrian oil   *New Tuscan oil*   *Ligurian oil*

Often, a dark green oil will have a strong, pungent flavor, but this is not always so. Nor is it true that lighter colored oils are always sweet; some can be quite peppery.

in an oil—a peppery bite and a pungent aftertaste? Or a sweet, rounded oil with fruity overtones? Think about what you will be serving it with. Perhaps you will need several different oils, each of which will match or contrast with your favorite dishes.

A wonderful vocabulary exists to describe the aromas and flavors of olive oil. Fruit and vegetable comparisons abound: the most common are almond, tomato, apple, pear, grass, and newly-mown hay. These refer only to hints of aroma, flavor, and aftertaste; the predominant taste should be of freshly pressed olives!

Olive oil has been used in the preparation of cosmetics and perfumes since ancient times. Greek cosmetics contained olive oil and were said to be good at preventing and attenuating wrinkles, fighting dandruff, and stopping hair loss. The Greeks also used olive oil as a body ointment and their athletes rubbed themselves with olive oil before entering the gymnasium or stadium, as did warriors before a battle. They taught these uses of oil to the ancient Romans and in their baths, aside from the frigidarium (cold bath), tepidarium (warm bath), and calidarium (hot bath), there was also a separate room for olive oil anointing, which was called the "bath of youth." In the first century AD, perfumes were also prepared with olive oil by adding musk and various aromas.

Below: olive oil is still used today in soaps, shampoos, conditioners, and various other cosmetics.

Storing Olive Oil

Like all fats, olive oil is a delicate product. It becomes rancid quite easily and needs to be stored carefully to preserve its flavor and health-giving properties. It should be stored in a clean, dry place, at temperatures between 58–64°F (14–18°C). There are two main problems to bear in mind when storing olive oil: it is easily "polluted" by other odors, and goes off relatively quickly.

When storing olive oil it is best to use opaque containers which are easy to clean and can be sealed.

An old Italian saying goes "Vino vecchio, olio nuovo" (old wine and new oil). Olive oil has a limited life span and should be consumed within a year of being made.

Olive oil absorbs other aromas and odors quickly and easily. This makes it an excellent base for essences and perfumes, not to mention aromatic oils (see pages 24–25). However, in the same way that it absorbs perfumes it will also take on any bad smells to which it is exposed. For this reason oil should always be kept in clean, odorless containers and stored in cupboards or rooms where it is not exposed to strong smells, such as smoke, paint, mold, or fuels. Some unfiltered oils create their own "pollution" in the form

In ancient times, olive oil was stored and transported in large terra-cotta amphorae (jars). Many of these jars carry seals and dates; at the palace of Knossos on the Mediterranean island of Crete, one can still see amphorae dating from the Minoan period (c.2200–1450 BC).

of sediment. Newly pressed oil sometimes looks slightly cloudy because of tiny pieces of sediment suspended in the oil. In time they will sink to the bottom and create a deposit which will then ferment, giving off an unpleasant odor that will pollute the oil. The best way to avoid this is to filter the oil within a month of its being made (this can be done at home by passing the oil through a piece of muslin). Filtering the oil will not impoverish it; in fact, it will add a frankness of flavor, and bring out its real perfumes.

Like many natural products, olive oil passes through a series of life stages. Newly pressed extra-virgin olive oil is often not well-balanced and can be "aggressive" and "disorganized" in aroma and flavor. It stabilizes about a month after production, acquiring harmony and its own special character. Month-old oil is at its peak; from then on it gradually relinquishes fragrance and vividness, becoming quite flat and tired by the end of the first year. After two years of life it is inedible and should be thrown out.

When buying olive oil make sure it is stored either in cans or tinted glass bottles. If it is in transparent glass it should come packaged in a box. When buying in large cans, decant it into smaller containers that can be sealed (green or brown tinted wine bottles are ideal for this). In the kitchen, take care not to leave your precious bottle of extra-virgin oil next to the stove – it will be spoiled by the heat. Finally, and it goes without saying (or should do), never store olive oil in the refrigerator.

Oil cruets are available in many beautiful and ornate shapes. Clear glass cruets are attractive on the table, but make sure the oil is not stored in them for long. Exposure to light will cause the oil to go rancid quite quickly.

17

Oil cruets were invented in France in the 17th century. The most classic type has two identical containers – one for oil and one for vinegar.

A simple oil cruet for everyday use on the table.

Serving Olive Oil

Every dining or restaurant table in Italy holds a shapely little bottle of olive oil, usually accompanied by a matching one containing vinegar, and salt and pepper shakers. Diners lavish the oil on salads, boiled vegetables, soups, pasta, bread, and a range of other foods too. Recently, a crop of trendier restaurants (and homes) have taken to serving olive oil in the bottle so that everyone can read the label and check that this is the most suitable oil for the dish they are eating. Like wine, the different oils should be matched with the food being served. The wrong oil can spoil a meal: for example, if you were to serve a very simple and delicate dish like boiled fish with a rough and tough Tuscan or Apulian oil their pronounced and peppery flavors would annihilate the fish's aroma and taste.

Tagliata (Serves 4)

Ingredients
- 1 lb/500 g sirloin steak, boned
- 8 oz/250 g fresh salad greens, preferably rocket
- salt and freshly ground black pepper to taste
- 4–6 tbsp extra-virgin olive oil

Cut the meat into thick slices. Place them over a very hot grill or under a broiler (or better still, a barbecue). When the meat is cooked on one side, turn and cook on the other. Transfer the meat to a chopping board and cut into slices about 1/8 in/3 mm thick. Arrange the rocket and sliced steak on a serving dish. Sprinkle with salt and pepper, drizzle with the olive oil and serve at once.

Wine: a dry, red (Chianti Classico)

Choosing the right oil

Sweet oils, like those from the area around Lake Garda, from Liguria, and many from Sicily and Sardinia, go well with fish, carpaccio (raw veal salad), and boiled vegetables. More piquant oils should be served with grilled red meats and vegetable soups and creams. Salads should be served with an oil that exults the fresh, slightly bitter taste of the greens. Personal taste is clearly an important factor here, but the basic rule is that the oil should not cancel out the flavors of the dish, but complement and enhance them.

Raw vegetables in olive oil dip
(Serves 6)

- 4–6 very young, fresh artichokes
- juice of 1 lemon
- 12 very fresh small carrots, preferably with their leaves
- 2 small, tender fennel bulbs
- 1 celery heart
- 12 radishes
- 6 scallions/spring onions
- ½ cup/125 ml extra-virgin olive oil
- salt and freshly ground black pepper
- good quality wine vinegar
- ½ cup/125 ml lemon juice

Only the freshest, most tender artichokes are suitable. Have one or two large, juicy lemon wedges ready to rub over all the cut surfaces as you work to prevent discoloration. Cut off the upper section of most of the leaves, leaving the fleshy, edible base of each leaf attached to the stem. Doing this will expose a central "cone" of leaves: slice about 1 in/2.5 cm off the top of this and part the leaves to gain access to the "choke," the spiny filaments which must be carefully trimmed away, leaving the fleshy, dish-shaped heart intact. Use a small sharp knife to scrape away the skin from the stalk; as each

artichoke is finished, drop it into a bowl of cold water acidulated with the juice of a lemon. Set aside for 15 minutes. If the carrots are very young and tender, scrub well and leave whole with a little of the stalk attached. If larger, peel and cut lengthwise into quarters. Discard the outermost layer of the fennel, cut the bulb from top to bottom, dividing it into quarters, and rinse well. Cut the celery heart lengthwise in half or quarters, wash and drain. Trim and wash the radishes, leaving any fresh, unwilted leaves attached. Trim the scallions, leaving only a short length of green leaf attached. Unless they are very fresh and firm, remove the outermost layer of the bulb. Be sure to

keep the scallions separate because if they touch the other vegetables they will spoil their delicate flavors. Drain the artichokes thoroughly and pat dry with paper towels. Arrange all the vegetables on a large serving platter. Place the platter in the middle of table and give each person a plate and a small bowl. Place containers of oil, vinegar, freshly squeezed lemon juice, salt, and pepper on the table and let each diner prepare their own bowl of dressing to dip the vegetables into. Serve with plenty of fresh bread.

Wine: a dry, sparkling white (Spumante di Vernaccia di San Gimignano)

Cooking with Olive Oil

Olive oil is one of the best cooking fats available. It is ideal for *soffritti* (sautéed garlic, onion, parsley, carrot, etc) which form the basis of so many Italian dishes. It is also excellent for roasting; for lighter roasts just rub a little oil directly onto the meat. If you are making roast potatoes, then you will need to use more oil so that they can turn crispy and a lovely deep gold (put fresh rosemary in with them for extra flavor).

Olive oil really comes into its own when frying foods. Eaten in moderation, fried foods are not bad for most people and they are so delicious! There are a few basic rules to follow which we have summarized in the box on the next page.

When frying, keep a slotted spoon on hand to remove pieces of food and batter from the oil. Tongs will also be useful to remove the food from the oil.

Opinions vary on whether you should use extra-virgin olive oil or just plain olive oil for frying. From a nutritional point of view, there is no difference between the two — they both reach smoking point (when dangerous substances are released) at a very high temperature, making them relatively healthy. From a taste point of view, the less flavorsome plain olive oil is best when cooking full-flavored foods, such as roast pork. Extra-virgin oil is the best choice when frying more delicately flavored foods, such as vegetables, since it will impart a little of its inimitable aroma to the finished dish. However, since best results are obtained by deep frying, and given the price of extra-virgin olive oil, plain olive oil will probably suffice on most occasions.

Tuscan Fried Mix

(Serves 4)

Ingredients
- ½ chicken, in pieces
- 2 calf's brains (optional)
- 4 lamb chops
- 1¼ lb/600 g potatoes, peeled and chopped
- 4 artichokes, cleaned and cut in quarters
- 2 zucchini/courgettes, cut in lengths
- 1 small cauliflower, in florets
- 6 eggs, beaten
- 1⅓ cups/200 g all-purpose/plain flour
- 3 cups/180 g bread crumbs
- 2 cups/500 ml olive oil, for frying
- dash of salt
- 1–2 lemons, cut in quarters or eights for serving.

Lightly boil the calf's brains (if using) and cauliflower florets. Drain well, then coat the calf's brains with the flour and dip in the egg. Heat the oil and fry until lightly browned. Drain on paper towels. Coat all the vegetables (except the potatoes) with flour then dip in the egg and fry until golden brown. Drain on paper towels. Finally, coat the lamb chops in flour, dip them in the egg, then dredge in the bread crumbs. Sprinkle with salt and serve as soon as possible after frying.

Wine: a dry red (Chianti Classico)

TIPS FOR SUCCESSFUL FRYING

To obtain perfect results when frying foods you will need a deep-sided skillet (frying pan), a slotted spoon, tongs (or two forks), and abundant olive oil. Fried dishes should be eaten hot; serve them as you cook or as soon afterward as possible.

- TEMPERATURE: Don't begin frying before the oil is hot enough. Ideal cooking temperatures are: *Medium* (275°F–300°F/130°C–150°C): ideal for pieces of raw food that need time to cook inside; *Hot* (300°F–325°F/150°C–160°C): ideal for precooked foods, croquettes, and to seal fillings in; *Very hot* (325°F–350°F/160°C–180°C): ideal for vegetables in julienne strips, leaves, or tiny pieces of food which require instant frying.
Initially, you may prefer to use a thermometer to gauge heat. Otherwise, check temperature by putting a small piece of the food you wish to cook in the oil to see how it reacts and adjust temperature accordingly. Temperature should never exceed 350°F/180°C. Don't wait until the oil is smoking; this is dangerous as it may catch fire (if it does, don't use water to extinguish it, just turn off the gas or electricity and cover the pan with a lid).

- Always use plenty of oil. The food should float. When you add it to the pan the whole surface should seal immediately against the oil. The less oil that enters the surface, the lighter and healthier the fried dish will be.

- Never use the same oil more than once. During cooking, keep the oil clean; if you leave tiny pieces of batter or food in the pan, they will burn and their acrid flavor will contaminate the taste of what you fry next. Keep the oil topped up to the same level during cooking.

- The food you want to fry should be at room temperature. If it is too cold, it will take longer to cook and absorb more oil.

- Don't put too many pieces in the pan at once. This will lower the temperature of the oil, increasing cooking time and causing food to absorb more oil. It may also stick together in a single unappetizing lump.

- If using a wire basket, heat it in the oil first to prevent the food from sticking to it.

Table Olives

About ten percent of the olives produced by the estimated 750 million olive trees around the globe are served as table olives. This means an annual production of around one million tons. Olives can't be eaten directly from the tree because they contain a very bitter, unpalatable substance called oleuropeina, which has to be eliminated first. In Italy, the process of preparing the fruit for the table varies from region to region and also changes according to the type of olive. Some olives are more suitable than others for the table, although in many regions the same varieties are used for making oil, cooking, and the table. The best table olives are medium to large in size (weighing about $\frac{1}{8}$ ounce/4 grams). They should be easy to pit with a ratio of at least 1 to 5 between the volume of pit and flesh. The higher this ratio is the more valuable the olives are. They should also have a low oil content, and an outer layer which is not too thick but still able to withstand the treatment process.

Tasty cured olives can be eaten al naturale straight from the jar, or used as a stuffing for chicken or other white meats.

22

Many green olives are preserved using the simple and very ancient method of keeping them in frequently changed cold water for about 10 days then transferring them to lightly salted water.

Table olives can be divided into two main types: green and black. Green olives are obtained from fruit that are picked early, before they turn black. They are harvested by hand, with care being taken not to scratch the surface. The best time to pick them is when they are just turning from dark to light green and the flesh is becoming less dense although it is not yet soft.

Black olives are picked when the fruit is almost fully ripe, just after they turn dark brown or black on the tree. There are many ways of preserving these olives; the large dark brown, almost violet colored ones known in Italy as "Greek" olives are picked as soon as they have changed color so that the skins don't wrinkle too much and the flesh doesn't become too soft. They are then placed in brine-filled containers where they begin to ferment. Further treatment includes the addition of vinegar and olive oil. These large, slightly bitter olives are perfect for salads. In a variation on this method, so-called *Kalamata* olives are prepared by making a cut in each olive so that it develops a sweeter taste. These olives are stored in oil and vinegar and then served with lemon rind.

Left: small, firm olives are the most suitable for dressing or stuffing. They can be served before dinner, together with a glass of wine or another aperitivo (pre-dinner drink). Most stuffed olives are filled with anchovies or bell peppers (capsicums) and then dressed with chopped garlic, parsley, and spicy red chilli peppers.

Dried black olives (above) look dark and wrinkly, almost as if they had no flesh. They are treated by being kept in water for a few days, then dried either under a hot sun or in the oven.

Gaeta olives (right) are kept in water for a few days, then packed in salt for 24 hours, then returned to water for about 40 days. They are then preserved in brine. These small brown olives are excellent for cooking, but their slightly bitter flavor also makes them good as table fare.

Large green olives (left) from Ascolana or Apulia are also treated in an alkaline solution, although it is usually a stronger one than for normal green olives.

Large, shiny black Baresane olives (right) are treated and preserved in much the same way as green olives.

Black olives in brine (left) are prepared throughout Italy in many different ways. They are usually made with small, black shiny olives and are often flavored with bay leaves.

Aromatic Oils

Using extra-virgin olive oil as the base for aromatic table oils is a relatively recent fashion. The first aromatic oil was made by adding a little chilli pepper, and this was soon followed by truffle-flavored oil. Thus began a race to see who could invent the tastiest and most original combinations. Purists have tended to shun the practice, claiming that a good oil will only get worse if combined with other ingredients. In a certain sense this is true, however, when made with care at home, aromatic table oils are fun to prepare and serve. They also make excellent and original gifts.

Chilli pepper oil

Ingredients
- 1 oz/30 g spicy red chilli peppers
- 2 cups/500 ml extra-virgin olive oil
- 1 bay leaf

Rinse the chilli peppers under cold running water. Dry thoroughly with paper towels. Finely chop the chilli peppers and add them to the olive oil with the bay leaf. Transfer the oil to a sterilized bottle and seal. Leave to infuse in a cool, dry place for about 30 days. Filter the oil. Add 2 or 3 whole chilli peppers to make it look more attractive. Place on the table and use to dress pasta, rice, fish, meat, and homemade pizzas. For a more delicate flavor, add fresh oil to the infused oil. For a spicier oil, leave to infuse for about 45 days.

Citrus-flavored oil

Ingredients:
- 2 cups/500 ml extra-virgin olive oil
- 1 orange
- 1 lemon

Scrub the fruit under cold running water with a soft brush. Use a lemon zester to peel the fruit. Add the zest (rind) to the olive oil and transfer to a sterilized bottle. Seal, and leave to infuse in a cool, dry place for about 2 weeks. Filter the zest from the oil. Use to dress salads or serve with fish and boiled or roasted meats.

Sage oil

Ingredients
- 10 sage leaves
- 2 cups/500 ml extra-virgin olive oil

Rinse the sage under cold running water and dry thoroughly with paper towels. Place the sage in a sterilized bottle and pour in the oil to cover. Seal, and leave to infuse in a cool, dry place for about 2 weeks. Filter the leaves from the oil (adding a few fresh ones to make it look attractive) and serve over salads, pasta, and soups.

Spiced oil

Ingredients:
- 4 cups/1 liter extra-virgin olive oil
- 2 bay leaves
- 2 cloves
- 6 mixed pepper corns
- 1 twig rosemary
- 4 juniper berries
- 1 piece of cinnamon
- 20 dried chilli peppers

Place all the ingredients in one or two bottles and cover with the oil.

Seal, and leave to infuse in a cool, dry place for about 30 days. Filter the herbs and spices from the oil (adding a few fresh ones to make it look attractive) and use for salads, boiled meats, or to marinate game. Vary the spices and herbs to suit your taste and the seasons.

Rosemary Oil

Ingredients:
- 2 cups/500 ml extra-virgin olive oil
- 2 twigs rosemary

Wash the rosemary carefully and dry well with paper towels. Place in a sterilized bottle and pour in the oil to cover. Seal, and leave to infuse in a cool, dry place for about 2 weeks. Filter the leaves from the oil (adding a few fresh ones to make it look attractive). Heat this oil before serving and use to flavor lamb, pork, and small game.

Wild fennel oil

Ingredients
- 2 cups/500 ml extra-virgin olive oil
- 3 twigs fresh wild fennel

Wash the fennel carefully and dry well with paper towels. Place the fennel in a sterilized bottle and pour in the oil to cover. Seal, and leave to infuse in a cool, dry place for about 30 days. Filter the leaves from the oil (adding a few fresh ones to make it look attractive) and serve with salads, pasta, and fish.

Preserved in Oil

Preserving food out of season or for times of want or famine has always been a challenge. Drying was probably the earliest form of preservation. Smoking food was another early method, as was conserving food in oil. However, it wasn't until the end of the 18th century that preserving food in glass jars or metallic containers became common. This prevented fermentation and the subsequent deterioration of the food product. This method was later developed into an art, a superb way of aromatizing and serving vegetables and a host of other foods. The choice of oil depends on the food being preserved: use a delicate oil for sweetish vegetables, and a stronger oil for more sapid ingredients.

Porcini mushrooms

- 2 lb/1 kg small firm porcini mushrooms
- 2 cups/500 ml white wine vinegar
- 2 cups/500 ml dry white wine
- 3 bay leaves
- 10 white pepper corns
- extra-virgin olive oil to cover
- salt to taste
- 10–15 leaves fresh mint, torn

Rinse and clean the mushrooms thoroughly, cutting off the earthy bottoms. Heat the vinegar, wine, pepper corns, and bay leaves in a saucepan and simmer the mushrooms for about 7 minutes. Drain well while still firm. Leave in a dry place for about 24 hours (they must lose all their humidity before going in the jars). Pack the mushrooms in sterilized jars and sprinkle each with a little salt and mint. Pour in enough oil to cover. Use a knife to make sure no pockets of air remain. Seal and store for at least a month before serving. White button mushrooms can also be prepared in this way.

Artichokes

- 24 small artichokes
- 2 cups/500 ml white wine vinegar
- 2 cups/500 ml water
- dash of salt
- 10 white pepper corns
- 3 bay leaves
- extra-virgin olive oil to cover

Clean the artichokes, cutting off the stalks and removing all the tough outer leaves so that only the tender hearts remain. Cut in half, removing the fuzzy choke inside. Heat the vinegar, pepper corns, and bay leaves in a saucepan and simmer the artichokes for 4–5 minutes. Drain well and pat dry with a clean cloth. Pack in sterilized jars and pour in enough oil to cover. Sprinkle with the salt. Use a knife to make sure no pockets of air remain. Seal and store for at least a month before serving.

Olive pâté

- 13 oz/400 g pitted green or black olives
- 6 tbsp extra-virgin olive oil
- salt and freshly ground white pepper

Finely chop the olives using a knife or food processor. Stir in enough of the oil to make a creamy paste. Transfer to sterilized jars, cover with oil, and seal. If liked, add herbs or spices, such as garlic or parsley, to the olives before chopping them. Serve this pâté on slices of warm toast or with pasta.

Sun-dried tomatoes

- 10 oz/300 g dried tomatoes
- extra-virgin olive oil to cover
- 4 anchovy fillets
- 1 tbsp capers
- salt and freshly ground black pepper
- dash of oregano

Soak the tomatoes in a little lightly salted boiling water for 4–5 minutes. Drain and dry on a clean cloth. Place the tomatoes in sterilized jars, alternating them with the anchovies, capers, and oregano. Pour in enough oil to cover the tomatoes and seal. Store for at least a month before serving.

Filled chilli peppers

- 24 small, round chilli peppers
- 24 anchovy fillets
- 24 capers
- extra-virgin olive oil to cover
- salt to taste
- dash of oregano

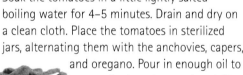

Clean and wash the chilli peppers, cutting off the end to remove the seeds. Simmer in boiling water for 1 minute, then drain well and dry. Fill each chilli pepper with an anchovy fillet wrapped around a caper. Pack the chilli peppers into sterilized jars, pour the oil over the top and seal. Store for at least a month before serving.

Anchovies

- 10 oz/300 g anchovies preserved in salt
- 1–2 tsp crushed chili pepper
- 1–2 tsp oregano
- extra-virgin olive oil to cover

Rinse the anchovies under cold running water, removing as much of the salt and scales as possible. Dry well then transfer to sterilized jars. Mix the chili pepper and oregano into the oil and pour over the anchovies. Seal the jars and store for at least a month before serving.

Eggplants

- 2 lb/1 kg eggplants/aubergines
- 2 cups/500 ml white wine vinegar
- 2 cloves garlic, peeled
- 2 tbsp finely chopped parsley
- 1 tsp dried oregano
- salt and freshly ground black pepper
- 1–2 tsp crushed chili pepper
- extra-virgin olive oil to cover

Rinse the eggplants and slice or dice them into cubes. Boil for 2–3 minutes in the vinegar flavored with the garlic. Drain and dry on a clean cloth. Place in large flat pan or dish and season with the parsley, oregano, salt, pepper, and chili pepper. Transfer to sterilized jars and pour in enough oil to cover. Seal and store for about a month before serving.

Bell peppers

- 1¾ lb/800 g red and yellow bell peppers/capsicums
- 3¼ cups/800 ml water
- juice of 1 lemon
- dash of salt
- 2 cups/500 ml white wine vinegar
- 10 black peppercorns
- 2 cloves garlic, thinly sliced
- 4 leaves fresh basil
- 1 tsp dried oregano
- extra-virgin olive oil to cover

Wash the bell peppers, cut them in half, and remove the seeds and core. Cut them in strips and cook in the water, lemon juice, salt, and pepper for about 4 minutes. Drain and dry on a clean cloth. Arrange them in sterilized jars with the basil, oregano, garlic, and a sprinkling of salt. Cover with the oil and seal. Store for at least a month before serving.

Zucchini

- 1¾ lb/800 g zucchini/courgettes
- 3¼ cups/800 ml white wine vinegar
- extra-virgin olive oil to cover
- 4 leaves fresh basil
- ½ tsp dried oregano
- 2 bay leaves
- 3 black peppercorns

Clean and rinse the zucchini, dry well and cut lengthwise in thin slices. Sprinkle lightly with salt and place in a colander to drain for about 3 hours. Boil for about 1 minute in the vinegar seasoned with the peppercorns and bay leaves. Drain well and dry on a clean cloth. Place in sterilized jars, alternating slices of zucchini with bits of basil leaves and a little oregano. Cover with the oil and seal. Store for at least a month before serving.

Uncooked Sauces

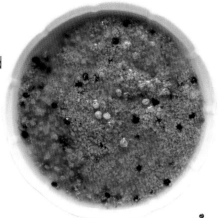

Extra-virgin olive oil is a key ingredient in many cooked sauces for pasta and meats. But it is in uncooked sauces that high quality extra-virgin olive oil really comes into its own. Cooking modifies the basic characteristics of the oil; but when uncooked, all its special character and flavor is left intact to enhance and exult the dish with which it will be served. Mayonnaise is a perfect example; nowadays, many recipes recommend using seed oils to maintain the yellow color of the eggs and to avoid the "bite" in the aftertaste that olive oil sometimes gives. However, the choice of the right type of olive oil, sweet and not too highly colored (Ligurian oil is ideal), makes a perfect mayonnaise.

Pepper sauce
- 1 slice of day-old bread
- 1 tbsp black pepper corns
- 1 tbsp red pepper corns
- 1 tbsp pink pepper corns
- 2 tbsp apple vinegar
- 4 tbsp extra-virgin olive oil

Crumble the bread and moisten it with the vinegar. In a food processor, grind the pepper corns. Then add the bread and oil. Continue mixing until the sauce is well mixed. Serve with roasted meats.

Mayonnaise

- 1¼ cups/300 ml extra-virgin olive oil (preferably from Liguria)
- 3 egg yolks
- dash of salt
- juice of ½ lemon

Beat the egg yolks with the salt until light and fluffy. Begin adding the oil very gradually, stirring all the time, to form a cream. When the mayonnaise is dense, stir in the lemon juice followed by the remaining oil. Store in the refrigerator.

Green sauce
- ¼ cup/30 g bread crumbs
- 3 tbsp red wine vinegar
- 3 tbsp chopped parsley
- 2 cloves garlic
- 1 hard-boiled egg
- 2 anchovy fillets
- 1 tbsp capers
- ½ cup/125 ml extra-virgin olive oil

Soak the bread crumbs in the vinegar for 2 minutes, then squeeze out excess moisture. Place in a blender with the parsley, garlic, anchovies, and capers and mix. Slowly add the olive oil as you mix. Serve with boiled meats or hard-boiled eggs.

Pecorino cheese sauce

- 2 tbsp parsley
- 10 basil leaves
- 1 tbsp pine nuts
- 1 hard-boiled egg
- 3 oz/90 g aged Pecorino cheese
- 4 tbsp extra-virgin olive oil
- salt and freshly ground black pepper

In a blender or food processor, blend the parsley, basil, and pine nuts. Add the hard-boiled egg, Pecorino, and olive oil. Mix well. Serve with white meats or poultry.

In the past, agresto was the juice of Agresta grapes (the small, firm, and slightly green grapes from the highest branches of the vine). Before tomatoes were introduced, they were widely used to flavor meats. Today they can be substituted with a sour grape juice.

Walnut sauce

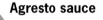

- 20 blanched walnuts
- 1 tbsp parsley
- 2 tbsp white wine vinegar
- 1 slice day-old bread (crust removed)
- 4 tbsp extra-virgin olive oil
- salt and freshly ground black pepper

Crumble the bread and moisten it with the vinegar. Chop the nuts in a food processor, along with the parsley. Add the bread and continue mixing, gradually adding the olive oil. Season with salt and pepper. Serve with fish or poultry.

Agresto sauce

- ½ cup/125 ml sour grape juice
- 1 tbsp onion, finely chopped
- zest of 1 orange
- salt and freshly ground black pepper
- 4 tbsp extra-virgin olive oil
- 1 slice day-old bread

Boil the grape juice until about two-thirds of it has evaporated, removing the foam that forms on top. Soak the bread in the hot juice. In a food processor or blender, finely chop the onion and orange zest. Add the soaked bread and continue to mix well. Gradually add the oil while whipping the mixture by hand with a fork. This sauce goes well with meat, poultry, or game.

Tarragon sauce

- 2 tbsp parsley
- 2 tbsp tarragon
- 2 cloves garlic
- 2 tbsp bread crumbs soaked in vinegar
- 4 tbsp extra-virgin olive oil

In a blender, chop the ingredients together, then gradually pour in the olive oil. This sauce will keep in the refrigerator for some time if covered with a thin coat of olive oil. Serve with boiled meats or fish.

Red sauce

- ¾ lb/750 g ripe tomatoes
- 2 cloves garlic
- 1 onion
- 5 basil leaves
- ½ tsp chilli pepper
- 1 tbsp vinegar
- salt
- 4 tbsp extra-virgin olive oil

Place the tomatoes in boiling water for 1–2 minutes, or until the skin starts to crack. Then place them in cold water for a couple of minutes. Dry and carefully remove the skins. Cut the tomatoes in half, remove the seeds, and place them cut-side down on a cutting board to drain. In a blender, chop the basil, garlic, and onion. Add the chilli pepper, vinegar, salt, and tomatoes. Blend well. Remove from the blender and use a fork to whip in the olive oil. Serve with boiled meats or poultry.

Pine nut sauce

- 1 slice of day-old bread
- 2 tbsp white wine vinegar
- 1 tbsp apple vinegar
- 1 tsp sugar
- 3 oz/90 g pine nuts
- 4 tbsp extra-virgin olive oil

Crumble the bread into small pieces and moisten it with the vinegars. In a mixer or food processor, finely chop the bread, sugar, and pine nuts, gradually adding the olive oil a little at a time. Serve with fish and poultry.

Olive Growing Areas

W ith the exception of the cool northwestern regions of Piedmont and Valle d'Aosta, the olive tree is cultivated throughout Italy. Apulia is the region with the highest output, followed by Calabria, Sicily, and Tuscany. There are over 395 different varieties of olive registered in the Italian index of olives, which makes the country a veritable mosaic of "cultivars." As with vines, there are both local varieties, which can only thrive and grow in specific microclimates, as well as versatile types, which yield good results in all sorts of terrain.

D.O.P. (Denominazione di Origine Protetta)

Awarded by the European Community, D.O.P. items are food or agricultural products typical of a particular area. They must be made with raw materials grown in the area, and transformed using methods and traditions not used elsewhere. The aim is to protect them against inferior or mass produced products and to provide consumers with a guarantee of their quality. Olive oil was one of the first food items to gain D.O.P. status. Every year new Italian oils gain the prestigious label.

ITALIAN D.O.P. OILS

DENOMINATION	REGION OF PRODUCTION	DENOMINATION	REGION OF PRODUCTION
RIVIERA LIGURE	Liguria	PENISOLA SORRENTINA	Campania
LAGHI LOMBARDIA	Lombardy	CILENTO	Campania
GARDA	Veneto, Lombardy, province of Trento	COLLINA DI BRINDISI	Apulia
		TERRA DI BARI	Apulia
BRISIGHELLA	Emilia Romagna	TERRA D'OTRANTO	Apulia
TERRE DEL CHIANTI CLASSICO	Tuscany	DAUNO	Apulia
UMBRIA	Umbria	LAMETIA	Calabria
SABINA	Lazio	BRUTIO	Calabria
CANINO	Lazio	MONTI IBLEI	Sicily
APRUTINO PESCARESE	Abruzzi	MONTE ETNA	Sicily
COLLINE TEATINE	Abruzzi	VAL DI MAZARA	Sicily
COLLINE SALERNITANE	Campania	VALLI TRAPANESI	Sicily

Vineyards, olive groves, fruit trees, cypresses, and oaks cover a large part of the Italian peninsula. Olive trees are typical of hill country that is not too exposed to the sun or bad weather conditions. Many of these trees are hundreds of years old and it can be quite moving when strolling in the Tuscan countryside to think that you may be sitting under the very tree that once cast its shadow over Michelangelo or Leonardo da Vinci.

This recipe is a classic all over Italy. It is served in homes and trattorias throughout the year. The sauce is suitable to serve with many different types of long and short pasta types, including penne, cavatappi, farfalle, spaghetti, spaghettini, linguine, and many more.

Tagliatelle with Uncooked Tomato Sauce
(Serves 4–6)

Ingredients
- 1½ lb/750 g cherry tomatoes
- 2 cloves garlic, finely chopped
- 1 small onion, finely chopped
- 8 basil leaves, torn
- ½ red chilli pepper, thinly sliced (optional)
- dash of salt
- 4 tbsp extra-virgin olive oil
- 500 g fresh tagliatelle pasta

Cut the tomatoes in half and pass them through a food mill to eliminate seeds and skins. Place the garlic, onion, basil, chilli pepper (if using), salt, and oil in a large bowl. Add the tomatoes and mix well. Cook the tagliatelle in a large pan of boiling, salted water until *al dente*. Drain well and transfer to the bowl with the sauce. Toss vigorously and serve at once.

Wine: a light, dry white (Tocai di Lison)

Liguria

Liguria's D.O.P. Riviera Ligure oil comes from the province of Imperia, where olive growing dates to around 1100 when it was introduced by Benedictine monks. Excellent oils are also produced on the Riviera dei Fiori, also in Imperia, the Riviera di Ponente in the province of Savona, and the Riviera di Levante in the provinces of Genoa and La Spezia. The leading variety of olive used in Liguria's olive oil production is the Taggiasca. It yields an oil known for its low acidity level, tenuous coloring, and delicate taste. Taggiasca's scent is mild but pleasant, with delightful dried fruit accents. In the past the milk-colored, lightly fruit-scented Biancardo was also produced from Taggiasca olives picked in April.

34

Mosto integrale

As suggested by its name (integral must), this oil is produced without the filtering process, which makes it far more aromatic and intense in flavor.

The Riviera dei Fiori

Liguria's most important production area is the Riviera dei Fiori, followed by the Savonese, which has similar but less well-known oils, and the Riviera del Levante.

Monocultivar Taggiasca

This oil is produced along the Ligurian coast with only one type of olive: the Taggiasca, also the most widespread on the territory.

Spaghettini with Raw Artichokes
(Serves 4)

Ingredients
- 8 small, fresh artichokes
- juice of 1 lemon
- salt and freshly ground black pepper
- 4 tbsp extra-virgin olive oil
- 1 lb/500 g spaghettini pasta
- 2 oz/60 g Parmesan cheese, in flakes

Clean the artichokes, cutting off the stalks, removing all the tough outer leaves, and slicing about 1 inch/2.5 cm off the tops. Cut in half, removing the fuzzy choke inside. Cut the artichokes into very thin slices. Place the slices in a bowl of cold water with the lemon juice and set aside for 15 minutes. Drain well, and dry carefully with a clean cloth. Place in a large serving bowl (large enough to hold the pasta too). Season with salt and pepper and drizzle with the oil. Cook the pasta in a large pan of boiling, salted water until *al dente*. Drain the pasta and toss with the artichokes. Drain well and transfer to the bowl with the sauce. Toss vigorously, sprinkle with the parmesan, and serve.

Wine: a light, dry white (Cinque Terre)

Terraced olive-growing
Much of the land in Liguria is steep hill country, and farmland is cut out of the hillsides. Many olive trees are grown in specially built, terraced groves.

Basil-flavored oil

Liguria has a mild climate where herbs like basil grow especially well. The delicate flavor of Ligurian oil makes an excellent base for basil-flavored oil. It is available commercially-made, but can also be made at home. Follow the instructions for Sage oil on page 24, replacing the sage leaves with twice as many fresh basil leaves.

Before the days of blenders, Basil sauce, called pesto in Italian, was made using a mortar and pestle. This beautiful example is cut from the tortured wood of a Ligurian olive tree.

Cooking with Ligurian oil

The sweet, delicate flavor of oil from Liguria goes best with fish and vegetables.

Reginette with Basil Sauce (Serves 4)

Ingredients
- 2 medium potatoes, diced
- 4 oz/125 g green beans, cut in lengths
- 1 lb/500 g reginette pasta
- 40 fresh basil leaves
- 1 tbsp pine nuts
- 3 tbsp freshly grated Parmesan cheese
- 2 tbsp extra-virgin olive oil
- 2 cloves garlic
- salt and freshly ground black pepper to taste

Bring a large pan of salted water to the boil and add the potatoes and beans. Boil for 2–3 minutes, then add the pasta. Meanwhile put the basil, pine nuts, cheese, oil, and garlic in a blender and mix to a smooth cream. Place in a large serving bowl (large enough to hold the pasta too). Drain the pasta and vegetables, keeping 3 tablespoons of the water to add to the sauce. Put the pasta, vegetables, and cooking water into the bowl with the sauce and toss vigorously. Serve hot.

Wine: a dry white (Vermentino)

Lombardy

Most of the olive oil produced in Lombardy comes from the province of Brescia, in the areas around lakes Garda and Iseo where the climate is milder than in the rest of the region. In the Garda area, the olive groves are located on hillsides of up to 2130 feet (650 meters), where average temperatures are above 70°F (20°C) in the summer and do not go below 32° F (0°C) in the winter. With their fruity bouquet and refined flavor, Garda's oils are of good quality. In the Iseo area olives are grown up to a height of 1640 feet (500 meters), as far north as the Val Camonica. They yield an exquisite, delicate oil, in minute quantities. Olive farming is also practiced on the shores of Lake Como, particularly near Bellagio. Since only a tiny amount of oil is produced most of it is consumed locally.

MAIN PRODUCTION ZONES: Lake Garda, Lake Iseo, Lake Como

MAIN OLIVE VARIETIES: Casaliva (Garda and Como lakes) ,Gargnà (Lake Garda), Leccino, Pendolino, Frantoio, Moraiolo

Cooking with oil from Lombardy
The bouquet of these oils are light and elegant but not too incisive. They are ideal for freshwater fish and light dressings.

Lemon-flavored "Garda Gold"
L'Oro del Garda, or Garda Gold, is a dressing based on an old recipe from the area. The best, newly harvested olives are pressed together with hand-picked lemons. The delicious oil has a deep, ongoing perfume and a delicate flavor. Just a few drops are enough to exalt the taste of a range of foods. Try it on fish or shellfish.

Pike in Olive Sauce
(Serves 4)

Ingredients:
- 2 lb/1 kg pike
- 7 oz/200 g bread crumbs
- ¾ cup/200 ml extra-virgin olive oil
- 3 tbsp finely chopped parsley
- 1 clove garlic, finely chopped
- salt and freshly ground black pepper to taste
- 1 tbsp white wine vinegar
- 3½ oz/100 g pickled vegetables, chopped
- 3½ oz/100 g green olives, pitted and chopped

Clean and eviscerate (gut) the pike. Rinse well and pat dry, then coat with the bread crumbs. Drizzle with a little of the oil and cook under a broiler (grill). Meanwhile, mix the parsley and garlic with the remaining oil and season with salt and pepper. Divide the pike into 4 portions and drizzle each one with the sauce, sprinkle with the vinegar, pickled vegetables, and olives, and serve.

Wine: a dry white (Riviera del Garda Bianco)

Trentino

MAIN PRODUCTION ZONES: *Lake Garda*

MAIN OLIVE VARIETIES: *Raza, Favarol, Rossanel, Leccino, Pendolino, Frantoio*

Trentino's cooler northern climate and harsh terrain is not especially well-suited to olive growing, most of which is concentrated in the milder microclimate in the vicinity of Lake Garda. Olive trees are grown up to a height of 1300 feet (400 meters) in the hills around the town of Riva del Garda at the northern tip of the lake. Only a small amount of oil is made in this region and almost all of it is consumed locally.

TRENTINO–
ALTO ADIGE

Trento

Riva del Garda

Lake Garda

Leek and Potato Soup
(Serves 4–6)

Ingredients
- 1 large onion
- small bunch of parsley
- 1 clove garlic
- 1 carrot
- 1 stalk celery
- 6 leeks
- 6 large potatoes
- 4 cups/1 liter cold water
- 6 leaves fresh basil
- 4 tbsp extra-virgin olive oil, plus extra for serving
- salt and freshly ground black pepper
- croutons (cubes of deep fried or toasted bread)

The Trentino Garda oil is very similar to the ones produced on the Lombardy side of the lake.

Finely chop the onion, parsley, garlic, carrot, and celery together. Sauté this mixture until tender (not golden) in the oil. Clean and slice the leeks. Peel and dice the potatoes. Add the leeks to the vegetables and cook for 10 minutes. Add the potatoes and water. Season with salt and pepper and add the basil. Cook until the potatoes are very tender. Remove from the heat. If a smooth creamy soup is desired, pass through a food mill or mix in a food processor. In winter, serve the soup piping hot poured over the croutons. In summer, chill the soup and serve with the croutons sprinkled on top. Drizzle with extra olive oil before serving.

Wine: a dry, aromatic white (Alto Adige Traminer Aromatico)

Veneto

VENETO

MAIN PRODUCTION ZONES: Verona province, Euganei and Berici hills

MAIN OLIVE VARIETIES: Grignan, Trep, Casaliva, Leccino, Frantoio, Pendolino. Rasara, Marzemino, Riondella, Matosso (Euganei and Berici hills)

As in other olive growing regions in northern Italy, production is confined to those areas with special climatic conditions. In the Veneto most olives are grown in the province of Verona, in the territory that lies between Lake Garda and the Valpolicella. Very little of the oil produced here is exported out of the region. An area providing extremely high quality oil is that of the Monte Grappa, between Marostica and Asolo, home of the exquisitely scented and softly flavored Leccino and Frantoio varieties. Here too, unfortunately, most of this oil is consumed locally.

Farfalle with Trevisian Radicchio and Caprino Cheese

(Serves 4)

Ingredients
- 1 onion, thinly sliced
- 7 tbsp extra-virgin olive oil
- 1 large head (or 2 small) Trevisian radicchio, cut in strips
- salt and freshly ground black pepper
- 4 tbsp light beer
- 4 oz/125 g soft fresh Caprino (goat's) cheese
- 2 tbsp milk

Sauté the onion in 3 tablespoons of the oil. When the onions are tender, add the radicchio and season with salt and pepper. Brown the mixture for a few minutes, then add the beer. When the beer is evaporated, add the Caprino and stir well, softening the mixture with the milk. Boil the pasta in a large pan of boiling, salted water until cooked *al dente*. Drain well and add to the pan with the sauce. Toss for a few minutes, drizzle with the remaining oil, and serve.

Wine: a dry red (Colli Berici Merlot)

Cooking with oil from the Veneto

With their elegant, light bouquet, these oils are ideal with vegetable dishes and soups. The slightly bitter taste of the region's radicchio (a red and white member of the chicory family), is beautifully set off by the local oils. If you can get radicchio, try liberally basting it with olive oil and baking or grilling.

Friuli-Venezia Giulia

In some areas of Friuli-Venezia Giulia, where a special microclimate occurs, olive farming dates back to the Roman era. Due to a spectacular frost that all but destroyed the olive groves towards the end of the 1920s, olive oil production was discontinued for an extended period of time. Production has resumed in recent years thanks to a group of devotees, and is rapidly expanding. From the Carso valley near Trieste, production has spread to the hill regions of Gorizia and Udine. Alongside traditional local varieties, new producers are attempting to grow the most sought after Italian olive types. Oil production is therefore very small, but of good timbre and personality, with richly accented fruit scents.

40

As well as or instead of olive oil, lard is often used for cooking purposes in this region, making for dishes with a more resolute character.

Mixed Greens Soup
(Serves 6)

Ingredients
- 1 leek
- 6 tbsp extra-virgin olive oil
- fresh wild fennel, about 3 stalks
- 8 oz/250 g mixed greens (turnip, radicchio, kale, Swiss chard), cut in strips
- 2 oz/60 g dried white cannellini beans (pre-soaked and then boiled with a sage leaf for 1 hour), plus cooking water
- salt and freshly ground black pepper
- 6 large slices firm-textured bread, toasted
- 2 oz/60 g freshly grated Parmesan cheese

Clean the leek and slice thinly. Fry in half the oil with the wild fennel. Add the mixed greens, cover and cook for about 10 minutes. Add the beans and the water they were cooked in. Season with salt and pepper and cover again. Cook for about 30 minutes on low heat. Place the toast in individual soup bowls and pour the soup over the top. Drizzle with the remaining oil, sprinkle with the cheese, and serve.

Wine: a light, dry red (Friuli-Colli Orientali Merlot)

Emilia Romagna

Once common in the hills around Bologna, today the olive tree is found only in two areas of Romagna, near Brisighella and on the Rimini hillsides. The most well-known oil is Brisighella, one of the select Italian varieties worthy of the D.O.P. label. Obtained almost exclusively from olives of the Nostrana di Brisighella variety, Brisighella is known for its very delicate, original aroma. Loose oil sales, while practiced in other areas, are uncommon in Romagna as production is almost entirely bottled and marketed.

Pasta with Raw Zucchini, Pecorino Cheese, and Mint
(Serves 4)

Ingredients
- 6 very fresh small zucchini/courgettes
- 1 tsp lemon juice
- salt and freshly ground black pepper
- 4 tbsp extra-virgin olive oil
- 6 fresh mint leaves
- 1 lb/500 g penne pasta
- 3 oz/90 g fresh Pecorino cheese, cubed

Cut the zucchini in julienne strips and place them in a bowl (large enough to hold the pasta as well). Add the lemon juice, salt, pepper, oil, and mint leaves. Stir well and let sit for about 20 minutes. Boil the pasta in a large pan of boiling, salted water until cooked *al dente*. Drain well and place in the bowl with the zucchini. Toss well, add the Pecorino cheese, toss again, and serve.

Wine: a light, dry red
(Sangiovese di Romagna)

You will sometimes be told that it is a good idea to add a few drops of olive oil to the water when cooking pasta to stop the pasta sticking together. This is an old wive's tale; if your pasta is sticking together during cooking it probably means you don't have enough water in the pan. You should also stir the pasta when you add it to the pot and from time to time during cooking.

Tuscany

TUSCANY

MAIN PRODUCTION ZONES: throughout the region

MAIN OLIVE VARIETIES: Leccino, Frantoio, Pendolino, Moraiolo, Maurino, Punteruolo (Versilia), Razzo (Pisan hills), Maremmano (province of Grosseto), Saggianese (Maremma hills), Caninese (Maremma)

Some of the best oils in Italy are produced in Tuscany. Olives are grown throughout the region, with the exception of the fertile plains and mountainous areas. In terms of olive growing, Tuscany can be divided into three distinct areas: the coastal strip, the Maremma region around Grosseto, and the inland hills. The coastal region's climate, though subject to vastly different temperatures, is influenced by its proximity to the sea. The overall quality is good, though diseases caused by insects jeopardize quality some years. In Maremma there are two varieties that define the character of the local oils: the Saggianese and the Caninese. However, the most important olive growing zone lies in the inland hills of Tuscany, in the provinces of Lucca, Pistoia, Prato, Firenze, Arezzo, and Siena. The oils obtained in each area can be vastly different, due to differences in climate, exposures, and soil composition, even when the varieties are identical. In recent years some growers have experimented with harvesting the different olive types separately, thus obtaining monovarietal oils. The first results have been encouraging, and the experiment continues.

42

With its straw wrapping, this jaunty Tuscan oil cruet (above) recalls the region's famous Chianti wine. The oils produced in the hills of the Chianti Classico region have an even more intense flavor than other Tuscan oils.

Laudemio

This oil is produced by a consortium of twenty-two Tuscan oil makers, according to strict regulations regarding soil types, harvesting times, and processing methods. Obtained from select olive groves of typical Tuscan varieties, Laudemio is an intense green color and has a fruity taste and smell, typical of fresh olives.

Human intervention

The olive growing area is quite varied in Tuscany, ranging from plains at sea level to heights of up to 2300 feet/700 meters. Even in areas that aren't particularly suitable for olive growing, such as the Sienese Crete (clay hills), or where climatic conditions are borderline, as in many inland hill regions, human intervention over the centuries has changed the landscape sufficiently so that superior quality olive oils can still be produced.

Tuscan Bread Salad
(Serves 4)

Ingredients
- 1 lb/500 g firm-textured bread, preferably unsalted, in slices or chunks
- 4 cups/1 liter cold water
- 1 cup/250 ml white wine vinegar
- 1 medium red/Spanish onion, thinly sliced
- ½ cup/125 ml extra-virgin olive oil
- salt and freshly ground black pepper
- 4 large salad tomatoes, cut into pieces
- 8–10 fresh basil leaves, torn

Soak the bread in the water and half the vinegar for at least 1 hour. Keep the onion in a little bowl with 2 tablespoons of the remaining vinegar for about 30 minutes. Squeeze the moisture out of the bread and transfer to a large bowl. Pour in the oil and the remaining vinegar and season with salt and pepper. Add the tomatoes, onion, and basil. Refrigerate for at least 1 hour before serving.

Wine: a young, dry red (Chianti)

Oil from Lucca

The area around Lucca yields some of the best oils in Tuscany. They tend to be sweeter and more delicately flavored than other Tuscan oils.

Cavolo nero, known as Tuscan kale or black cabbage in English, is a tall leafy member of the cabbage family. It is a specialty of Tuscany.

Cooking with Tuscan oil

Extremely popular for its intense fruity aroma, grassy scent, and spicy, bitterish flavor, Tuscan oils go particularly well with garbanzo beans (chick peas), Florentine beef steak, and tasty vegetables like broccoli.

Ribollita
(Serves 6)

Ingredients
- 1 red/Spanish onion, finely chopped
- 4 tbsp extra-virgin olive oil
- 10 oz/300 g dried cannellini beans, pre-soaked and boiled in salted water with a sage leaf for 1 hour
- 3 cups/750 ml beef stock (homemade or stock cube)
- ½ small Savoy cabbage, shredded
- 3 small tomatoes, coarsely chopped
- 8 oz/250 g Swiss Chard, shredded
- 1 zucchini/courgette, coarsely chopped
- 1 carrot, cut in wheels
- 1 celery stalk, coarsely chopped
- 2 potatoes, diced
- 8 oz/250 g Tuscan kale, shredded
- 1 leek, cut in wheels
- salt and freshly ground black pepper to taste
- 6 slices firm-textured bread

Sauté the onion in half the oil. Purée two-thirds of the cannellini beans in a blender. Add the puréed beans and stock to the onion. Add all the vegetables and cook until tender. Stir in the rest of the beans, and season with salt and pepper. Arrange the bread in an oiled baking dish then pour the vegetable soup over the top. Drizzle with the remaining oil and bake in a preheated oven at 400°F/200°C/gas 6 for 30 minutes. Serve hot.

Wine: a dry red (Chianti dei Colli Fiorentini)

All traditional Tuscan recipes include oil. There are even some cookies and cakes that are made with oil instead of butter.

Tomato and Bread Soup
(Serves 4)

Ingredients
- 4 whole cloves garlic, peeled
- 4 tbsp extra-virgin olive oil, plus extra for serving
- 14 oz/450 g canned tomatoes
- 12 leaves fresh basil, torn
- 10 oz/300 g firm-textured, day-old bread, cut in thick slices and diced
- 1¼ cups/300 ml boiling water

Sauté the garlic in the oil. When the garlic begins to soften, crush the cloves with a fork. When it begins to turn gold, remove it. Add the tomatoes, breaking them up with a wooden spoon. Cook over low heat until the tomatoes reduce. Add the basil and stir in the bread. Add about half the water and turn up the heat. Stir often, adding more water as required to obtain a thick porridge-like consistency. Turn off the heat and let the soup sit for 5 minutes before serving. Serve warm with a drizzle of extra-virgin oil on top.

Wine: a dry red (Chianti dei Colli Fiorentini)

All three soups in this chapter on Tuscany are made using the local firm-textured, unsalted bread. Bread without salt has been produced in Tuscany for centuries. After the medieval poet Dante was expelled from his native city of Florence for political intrigue, he lamented in the Divine Comedy "O quanto è salato il pane altrui." (How salty other people's bread is).

The Marches

Some excellent extra-virgin oils are produced in the Marches. One, made from Frantoio and Leccino olives, is favored by the Bora wind which blows across the Adriatic Sea. Light green in color, its fragrant, not overly fruity flavor goes well with vegetable soups. Another very good extra-virgin oil is produced in the area around Ancona. Its delicate aroma suggests hazelnuts and straw, while its flavor is surprisingly intense and fruity. It is made with Carboncella, Raggiolo, and Frantoio olives. Most oils produced in this region go very well with fish and seafood.

This dish requires time and patience but these delicious little olives are so good that you will be tempted to make them again and again.

46

ASCOLANA OLIVES
The Marches is also known for its production of table olives. The Ascolana variety is among the best in Italy. The oil made from Ascolana olives is yellowy green in color and is delicate and almost sweet in flavor.

Stuffed, Fried Olives
(Serves 6)

- 5 oz/150 g minced beef
- 5 oz/150 g minced pork
- 2 tbsp extra-virgin olive oil
- 2 tbsp tomato paste
- 3½ oz/100 g chicken livers, chopped
- 1 day-old bread roll
- 3 eggs
- 5 tbsp freshly grated Parmesan cheese
- salt and freshly ground black pepper
- dash each of nutmeg and cinnamon
- 60 giant green olives, pitted
- 1 cup/150 g all-purpose/plain flour
- 5 oz/150 g bread crumbs
- 2 cups/500 ml olive oil, for frying

Sauté the beef and pork in a skillet (frying pan) with the extra-virgin oil for 5 minutes. Add the tomato paste and cook for 15 minutes. Add the chicken livers and cook for 5 minutes more. Soak the bread roll in cold water, squeeze out excess moisture, and crumble. In a bowl, combine the meat mixture with the bread, 1 egg, the Parmesan, salt, pepper, nutmeg, and cinnamon. Mix well and then stuff the olives. Arrange three bowls, the first with the flour, the second with the remaining eggs (beaten), and the third with the bread crumbs. Dredge the olives in the flour, dip them in the egg, and then in the bread crumbs. Deep-fry in a skillet with the frying oil. When a crisp, golden crust forms around each olive, remove with a slotted spoon. Place on paper towels to drain. Serve hot.

Wine: a dry red (Rosso Piceno)

Umbria

UMBRIA

MAIN PRODUCTION ZONES: hills around
Lake Trasimeno, the Umbra valley
MAIN OLIVE VARIETIES: Dolce Agogia,
Moraiolo

The production of olive oil in Umbria is important both in terms of quantity and quality. So much so that the region is sometimes called the "Gold Coast" of Italian olive farming. The oil-making tradition began with Etruscan colonization sometime before the 7th century BC and was strengthened during the Roman era. The main olive-growing areas are the Trasimeno hills and the Umbra valley. The former is the home of the Dolce agogia variety, which produces light and refined oils of medium fruitiness. In the Umbra valley, where Moraiolo is the most common variety, the oils are intensely fruity, with hints of artichoke and bitter almonds in their flavor and aftertaste.

Cooking with Umbrian oils

Umbria's well-balanced oils are highly versatile and can be used with a wide variety of Italian dishes.

Spelt is a very ancient Mediterranean grain which has come back into fashion in the past decade. If you can't find it locally, replace with an equal quantity of pearl barley.

47

Spelt and Vegetable Soup
(Serves 6)

Ingredients
- 1 onion, chopped
- 2 cloves garlic, finely chopped
- 1 carrot, 1 stalk celery, 1 leek, chopped
- 4–6 tbsp extra-virgin olive oil
- 4 oz/125 g pancetta, diced
- 10 oz/300 g spelt, soaked in salted water overnight
- 10 oz/300 g dried cannellini beans, pre-soaked, boiled in salted water with sage
- salt and freshly ground black pepper

Sauté the onion, garlic, carrot, celery, and leek in half the oil until soft. Add the pancetta and cook until golden. Add the spelt and cook, stirring for 5 minutes.

Remove from heat and purée in a blender, together with two-thirds of the cannellini beans. Add the puréed beans and some of their cooking water to the spelt mixture. Cook over low heat, adding extra bean water if necessary, until the spelt is cooked. Add the rest of the beans and cook for 5 minutes more. Let the soup rest for 10 minutes, drizzle with the remaining oil, and serve.

Wine: a dry white (Orvieto Classico)

Lazio

MAIN PRODUCTION ZONES: Sabina, province of Viterbo

MAIN OLIVE VARIETIES: Carboncella, Raja, Moraiolo, Frantoio (Sabina), Rosciola (Sabina and province of Frosinone), Caninese (Canino), Itrana (province of Latina)

Lazio can boast two areas that have obtained the D.O.P. label: Sabina, in the provinces of Rome and Rieti, and Canino in the province of Viterbo. These are the traditional zones for high-quality oil production, although in recent years other areas in the south of the region, in the Latina and Frosinone provinces, have also produced some excellent oils. The D.O.P. Sabina oil has a fresh fruit aroma and an aromatic and intense flavor. The Canino oil, produced in the northwest, near Lake Bolsena, also has a fruity aroma with herb accents. In Latina, the Itrana olives produce oils with a distinctively floral fragrance. Frosinone yields sweet oils, prevalently made from Rosciola olives.

Canino oil is named after the chief cultivar in its make up, the Caninese.

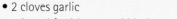

Bruschetta with Tomato and Basil
(Serves 4)

Ingredients:
- 4 large slices firm-textured bread
- 2 cloves garlic
- salt and freshly ground black pepper
- 8 tbsp extra-virgin olive oil
- 6 ripe tomatoes
- 8–12 fresh basil leaves, torn

Toast the bread and rub it with the garlic. Sprinkle with salt, pepper, and half the oil. Cut the tomatoes in half. Scoop out all the seeds, sprinkle with salt, and set them upsidedown for 20 minutes to drain. Chop the tomatoes in small cubes. Arrange them on the toast and garnish with the basil. Drizzle with the remaining oil and serve. Bruschetta makes a healthy after school snack and a great appetizer. Add a little diced mozzarella cheese to enrich it.

Wine: a light, dry white (Colli Albano)

Besides fresh tomato bruschetta, there are countless other versions, made with tomato sauce, sliced onion, pepper, basil, and other dressings. In Tuscany (where bruschetta is known as fettunta), boiled black cabbage or white cannellini beans are traditional toppings.

48

Abruzzi

Olives are grown throughout the Abruzzi region. One of the best oils (it bears the prestigious D.O.P. label) is produced in the provinces of Teramo and Pescara, especially in the area around the towns of Pianella, Moscufo, and Loreto Aprutino. It is made with the local Dritta olives, which many claim are the best in Italy for oil. Their oil is bright green with an intense and fruity aroma and a rich flavor. The most important olive growing area lies further south, in the Sulmona basin and the Tirino valley. The main varieties here are the Leccino, Toccolana, Moraiolo, and Frantoio. The Gentile di Chieti variety is also gaining ground thanks to efforts to promote local varieties.

Mushroom soup
(Serves 4)

Ingredients
- 1¼ lb/600 g porcini mushrooms
- 2 cloves garlic, finely chopped
- 2 tbsp parsley, finely chopped
- 3 tbsp extra-virgin olive oil
- ¾ cup/200 ml white wine
- 2 cups/500 ml water or vegetable stock
- 1 tsp dried calamint or thyme
- salt and freshly ground black pepper
- 4 large slices firm-textured bread, toasted

Trim the mushrooms and rinse carefully under cold running water. Dry well and chop coarsely. Sauté the garlic and parsley in the oil in a large, heavy-bottomed pan. Add the mushrooms and cook over high heat for 3–4 minutes. Pour in the wine and cook until it has evaporated. Lower the heat to medium and pour in the water or stock. Season with the calamint, salt, and pepper and cook until the mushrooms are tender. Place a slice of toast in each serving bowl and pour the soup over the top. Serve hot.

Wine: a dry red (Montepulciano d'Abruzzo)

Molise

This diminutive region plays host to a long-standing and thriving olive growing tradition. Most oil is produced in the Biferno valley, in the area around Larino. Made using the local Gentile di Larino olives, this oil is green with yellowy lights. Its delicate aroma is backed by a full, smooth flavor with a hint of almonds in the aftertaste. In other areas, olive varieties from Apulia, including Coratina, Peranzana, and Cellina, are common. Growers in Molise have been successful in recent years in raising the overall quality of the oils produced.

50

Cooking with oil from Molise
Molise's versatile oils are generally sweet tasting, with floral and fruit overtones in their scent. They are best when served with pasta and lamb.

Penne with Ricotta
(Serves 4)

Ingredients
- 10 oz/300 g fresh Ricotta cheese (ewe's cheese)
- dash of nutmeg
- 1 tbsp grated lemon zest
- 2 tbsp freshly grated Parmesan cheese
- 4 tbsp extra-virgin olive oil
- 1 lb/500 g penne pasta
- salt and freshly ground black pepper

Put the Ricotta in a bowl large enough to hold the pasta as well. Stir in the nutmeg, lemon rind, Parmesan, and oil. Boil the pasta in a large pan of salted boiling water until cooked *al dente*. Add about 2 tablespoons of the pasta water to the ricotta, then season with salt and pepper. Drain the pasta and add to the Ricotta mixture. Toss well and serve.

Wine: a light, dry white (Biferno Bianco)

Campania

Campania's excellent climate and wealth of varieties of olive provide the region with ideal conditions for making oil. In terms of total output, it is Italy's fifth oil producing region. Not all the oils are of equal quality, but some excellent ones are produced on the Sorrento peninsula and in Cilento. Some of the olive groves along the coast in the Pisciotta area are reputed to contain trees with a median age of 1200 years! The extra-virgin oil produced on the Sorrento peninsula, made with Frantoio and Leccino olives, has an intense aroma of Mediterranean herbs and a full fruity flavor. Another excellent oil is produced at Sannio using Racioppella and San Lorenzo maggiore varieties, among others.

MAIN PRODUCTION ZONES: province of Salerno, Cilento, Sorrento peninsula, Sannio

MAIN OLIVE VARIETIES: Rotondella (province of Salerno and Cilento), Carpellese (province of Salerno), Minucciola (Sorrento peninsula), Pisciottana, Salella (Cilento), Leccino, Coratina, Frantoio, Carolea

Cooking with oil from Campania

These oils are best with meat, fish, or as a base for fish soup.

Ischia-Style Rabbit
(Serves 4)

Ingredients
- 1 rabbit, weighing about 3 lb/1.5 kg, preferably with the liver
- juice of 1 lemon
- 4 cloves garlic, chopped
- ¾ cup/200 ml extra-virgin olive oil
- ¾ cup/200 ml dry white wine
- 1½ lb/750 g tomatoes, peeled and chopped
- salt and freshly ground black pepper
- 6–8 sprigs fresh rosemary

Rinse the rabbit and divide it into about 8 pieces. Remove the liver and wash in a little cold water mixed with the lemon juice. Sauté the garlic in the oil for 2–3 minutes. Add the rabbit and sauté until lightly browned. Pour in the wine and cook until it has evaporated. Add the tomatoes and season with salt and pepper. Cook over medium heat for about 20 minutes. Chop the liver coarsely and add to the pan with the rosemary. Cook over high heat for 5 minutes then serve.

Wine: a light, dry white (Biferno Bianco)

Basilicata

Squeezed in between Campania, Apulia, and Calabria, Basilicata is divided into just two provinces – Potenza and Matera. Although the economy of the region is based on agriculture, difficult soil conditions, low rainfall, and the number of hills, make any sort of farming a challenge. However, olives have been grown here for centuries and there are innumerable local varieties. Maiatica di Ferrandina, Palmarola, Angellina, Ripolese, and Giamara are probably the best. The oils produced are golden yellow in color, with a delicate aroma and an intense and penetrating flavor.

MAIN PRODUCTION ZONES: *Metaponto, Vulture, Basento valley*

MAIN OLIVE VARIETIES: *Maiatica di Ferrandina, Palmarola, Angellina, Ripolese, Giamara*

Beans on Toast
(Serves 6)

- 1 lb/500 g dried white cannellini beans
- salt and freshly ground black pepper
- 3–4 leaves fresh sage
- 12 slices densely-textured bread, toasted
- 6 tbsp extra-virgin olive oil

Soak the beans in water for 12 hours. Boil in plenty of salted water with the sage for 1½ hours. Arrange 2 slices of toast on individual serving dishes and top with the beans, adding some of the cooking water as well to soften the bread. Drizzle with the oil and pepper and serve.

Wine: a dry red (Aglianico del Vulture)

Cooking in Basilicata

Known in Italy as *cucina povera* ("poor cooking"), Basilicata cuisine is simple and based on traditions that stretch back thousands of years. Bread, pasta, pulses, cheese, olives, pork, lamb, and fish form the basis of the diet. Typical Mediterranean fare, these dishes are all enhanced by the local oil.

Apulia

Apulia's olive farming is one of Italy's greatest agricultural resources: almost 40 percent of the country's total, about 20 percent of the European Community's, and 12.5 percent of worldwide output are grown here. There are three main growing areas: Bari, Foggia, and the Salento peninsula. In the Bari province, the most intensive farming area is in Murge where the trees, often centuries old, are placed in vases and grown together with almond trees and vegetables. In the Foggia province, olive farming is practiced on the gentle slopes of the upper Tavoliere, in the Gargano, and also in the Dauno area. Half of Apulia's entire production comes from the Salento peninsula. Until recently however, most of the oil produced in Apulia was not especially good and the emphasis was placed more on quantity than quality. This is changing rapidly as the fact that there are now four D.O.P. oils produced in Apulia shows.

APULIA

MAIN PRODUCTION ZONES: throughout the region

MAIN OLIVE VARIETIES: Coratina (province of Bari, province of Foggia), Ogliarola Barese (province of Bari), Cima di Mola (province of Bari), Peranzana (upper Tavoliere), Ogliarola Garganica (Gargano), Ogliarola (pre-Appennino Dauno, Salento), Rotondella (pre-Appennino Dauno), Gellina di Nardò (Salento)

Bitonto oil

An excellent extra-virgin oil is produced at Bitonto, in the the province of Bari. Greeny-gold in color, it has a full, almost sweet flavor, with a hint of almonds in the aftertaste. According to local legend, Aristeo, God of the earth and its fruits, introduced the olive tree to the Bitonto region.

THE TASTE OF APULIA
There are so many different oils made in Apulia that it is very difficult to generalize. Apulian oils can be peppery and intense, ideal for enhancing the spicy local dishes; but they can also be rounded, mature, salty, and even sweet.

Terra di Bari

This is one of Apulia's four D.O.P. oils. This area's oils are of excellent quality, with a full-flavored taste that perfectly complements local dishes.

OLIO
EXTRA
VERGINE
di OLIVA

D.O.P.
Denominazione di Origine Protetta

TERRA
DI BARI

BITONTO

Reg. CE 2081/92

0.75 litro ℮

This dish, called 'ncapriata in Italian, hails from ancient Roman times when it was fed to hungry soldiers. An almost identical dish is still prepared in Egypt.

Apulia is a prime vegetable growing region and they make up an important part of the diet. In the local tradition, a meal will often end with a platter of raw carrots and celery (or whatever else is in season) and a bowl of delicious olive oil to dip them into and munch on.

Fava Bean Purée
(Serves 4)

Ingredients
- 10 oz/300g dried fava beans/ broad beans
- 1 celery stalk, chopped
- 1 large potato, chopped
- 2 medium onions, chopped
- dash of salt
- 6 tbsp extra-virgin olive oil
- 1 lb/500 g boiled chicory (or spinach)
- whole or crushed chilli peppers, as liked

Soak the fava beans overnight. Drain and rinse well then put them in a pot with the celery, potato, and onions. Cover with water and simmer over low heat for 2 hours. Season with salt and add half the olive oil. Pass the mixture through a food mill (or blend) to form a purée. Heat 1 tablespoon of the oil in a saucepan and add the purée. Cook for 5 minutes. Ladle into individual soup bowls and top with the chicory and chilli peppers and drizzle with the remaining oil. Serve hot.

Wine: a light, dry white (Lizzano Bianco)

Beef rolls, Bari-style
(Serves 4)

Ingredients
- 12 thin slices of veal
- 2 cloves garlic, finely chopped
- 2 tbsp finely chopped parsley
- 7 oz/200 g Pecorino cheese, cut in small cubes
- ½ onion, finely chopped
- 2 tbsp extra-virgin olive oil
- 3 bay leaves
- salt and freshly ground black pepper
- 1 lb/500 g canned tomatoes

Lay the slices of veal out on a clean work surface. Sprinkle with the garlic and parsley followed by the cheese. Roll the veal up and hold in place with a toothpick. Sauté the onion in the oil with the bay leaves. Add the veal rolls and cook over medium heat for about 5 minutes. Season with salt and pepper. Pour in the tomatoes, partly cover the skillet (frying pan) and cook until the tomatoes reduce and the meat is tender (20–30 minutes). Serve hot.

Wine: a dry red (Salice Salentino Rosso)

COOKING WITH APULIAN OILS
Given the variety of oils available and their traditional place in Apulian cooking, there really are oils for every occasion. Raw or boiled vegetables dressed with local oil are a must. Soups and pasta with fish are also excellent.

MIXED CULTIVATION
In some areas of Apulia, olive trees are grown together with almond trees, and assorted vegetables.

Calabria

MAIN PRODUCTION ZONES: *throughout the region*

MAIN OLIVE VARIETIES: *Carolea, Sinopolese, Ottobratica, Grossa di Gerace*

Olive groves cover the greater part of the cultivated area of Calabria and the region is the second largest olive oil producer in Italy. About a third of its output is high quality extra-virgin oil, while the rest is the less distinguished, plain olive oil. Much of the extra-virgin oil is of outstanding quality and the region boasts two prestigious DOP (Denominazione di Origine Protetta, meaning "of protected origin") oils – Lametia and Bruzio. The olives are grown in single-variety groves, with a series of accurately controlled procedures that give rise to an end product which has a unique, long-lasting flavor brimming with the intense bouquet of the Mediterranean.

Cosenza

Lamezia Terme

Catanzaro

Reggio di Calabria

Much of Calabria is arid and mountainous, but the fertile valleys are dedicated to citrus fruit farms, market gardening (tomatoes, bell peppers, eggplants/aubergines), and olives. Herbs grow wild in the hills and fish are plentiful along the coasts. Local cuisine is based on these quintessentially Mediterranean products.

Marinated Anchovies with Mint
(Serves 4)

Ingredients
- 24 fresh anchovies
- ⅔ cup/100 g all-purpose/plain flour
- 1 cup/250 ml olive oil for frying plus 2 tbsp extra-virgin olive oil to serve
- bunch of fresh mint
- 2 tbsp white wine vinegar
- dash of salt

Clean and wash the anchovies, removing their backbones. Dry well and coat with flour, shaking off any excess. Heat the olive oil until very hot (but not smoking), then add the sardines. Fry for a few minutes until cooked through, then drain on paper towels. Place the sardines in a shallow serving dish. Sprinkle with salt, then drizzle with the vinegar. Arrange the mint leaves attractively on top. Set aside for 24 hours. Drizzle with the extra-virgin oil just before serving.

Wine: a light, dry white (Melissa Bianco)

Sicily

Olive farming in Sicily was begun by the Greeks, continued by the Romans, and consolidated during the Arab reign in the Middle Ages. Sicilian oil ranks highly both in terms of quantity (it is the third oil-producing region in Italy), and quality. Most of the main varieties of Sicilian olives can be used to make oil and as table olives and the island boasts a wide range of excellent products in both sectors. Generally speaking, olives are harvested earlier in Sicily, usually in October. The most interesting olive farming areas are the Trapani province, the area around Etna, and the Iblei Mountains. Etna's oils can be recognized for their appetizing greeny-yellow hue, refined fruity aroma, and slightly bitter, spicy flavor. The Iblei Mountains are in the Siracusa province of southern Sicily. The groves themselves are situated well up the mountains because of the high summer temperatures. The Iblei oils have great personality and refinement, with a fresh tomato fragrance.

SICILY

MAIN PRODUCTION ZONES: province of Trapani, area of Mount Etna, Iblei Mountains

MAIN OLIVE VARIETIES: Nocellara del Belice e Cerasuola (Trapani), Nocellara Etnea (Etna), Brandofino (Alcantara Valley), Tonda Iblea e Moresca (Iblei Mountains)

Orange Salad
(Serves 4)

Ingredients
- 4 juicy oranges
- salt and freshly ground black pepper
- 10 black olives, pitted and cut in half
- 1 small white onion, thinly sliced
- 4 tbsp extra-virgin olive oil

Peel the oranges, taking care to remove all the white pith. Slice thinly and place in a salad bowl. Sprinkle with a little salt, then add the olives and onion. Drizzle with the oil and season with a generous grinding of pepper. Serve as a starter.

Wine: a light, dry white (Bianco di Donnafugata)

Taste

Contrary to what one might assume, many Sicilian oils are sweet and delicate, though richly scented. Others can be as strong and peppery as their Tuscan cousins to the north.

Sicilian landscape

Olive groves set at higher altitudes are less subject to scorching summer temperatures, providing ideal conditions for the production of light and elegant oils. Table olives are delicious and plentiful in the picturesque Vucciria market in Palermo.

Sicilian Pesto
(Serves 4)

Ingredients
- 2 tbsp capers, salted
- 1¾ lb/750 g ripe tomatoes
- dash of salt
- 4 tbsp extra-virgin olive oil
- 1 tsp crushed chilli pepper
- 1 clove garlic, finely chopped
- 1 tsp dried oregano
- 1 lb/500 g pipette rigate (or similar) pasta

Rinse the capers under running cold water for 1–2 minutes to remove some of the salt. Dry well. Wash the tomatoes, then cut them in half. Use a knife to remove the seeds. Sprinkle with a little salt and lay them upside down on a cutting board to drain for about 30 minutes. In a bowl (large enough to hold the pasta later), mix the oil, chilli pepper, capers, garlic, and oregano. Cut the tomatoes in cubes and add them to the mixture. Refrigerate for about 1 hour. Finally, boil the pasta in a large pan of salted, boiling water until cooked *al dente*. Drain and add to the bowl with the sauce. Toss well and serve.

Wine: a dry white (Alcamo)

Pasta with roasted bell peppers makes a refreshing summer meal. The sweet and sour flavors are typically Sicilian and reflect the influence of Middle Eastern cooking on the region. Be careful not to overcook the pasta; as soon as it is cooked al dente, drain in a colander and place under cold running water to stop the pasta cooking any further. Dry well and mix in with the sauce. This dish can be prepared in advance. Take it out of the refrigerator about 30 minutes before serving.

The valleys of Trapani

The valleys of Trapani in western Sicily yield excellent oils, with fresh fruit and herb scents reminiscent of artichokes and tomato leaves.

Roast Bell Pepper Pasta Salad

(Serves 4)

Ingredients
- 6 large bell peppers/capsicums (red and yellow)
- 4 tbsp extra-virgin olive oil
- salt and freshly ground black pepper to taste
- 2 tbsp capers
- 2 anchovy fillets, crumbled
- 1 tbsp raisins, soaked in warm water
- 1 tbsp pine nuts
- 1 lb/500 g rigatoni (or similar short pasta)

Roast the bell peppers over the flame of a gas stove or under a broiler (grill) until their skins are blistered and black all over. Transfer to a brown paper bag, close tightly and leave for 10–15 minutes (this loosens the skins further and makes peeling easier.) When they are cool enough to handle, peel off the skin with your fingers. Cut the bell peppers in half, remove the stems and seeds, then cut the soft flesh into thin strips lengthwise. Arrange them on a large shallow dish. Mix the olive oil, salt, pepper, capers, anchovy, raisins, and pine nuts and spread this mixture over the bell peppers. Leave for about 30 minutes. Cook the pasta in a large pan of salted boiling water until cooked *al dente*. Drain and place under cold running water to stop the cooking process. Drain again and dry in a clean cloth. Transfer to a serving dish. Add the bell peppers and toss well. Serve at room temperature.

Wine: a dry rosé (Etna Rosato)

Sardinia

Conditions on the beautiful Mediterranean island of Sardinia are perfect for growing olives and they thrive in every province. The island's isolation has helped to preserve the autonomous cultivars (native varieties) that so distinguish Sardinian oils, providing them with their original flavors and scents. In recent years Sardinian olive farmers have started picking the olives earlier and taking more care over the pressing process; this, combined with the island's natural advantages, has led to some great oils that showcase the local varieties' excellent qualities, such as their trademark floral scents.

60

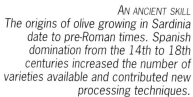

AN ANCIENT SKILL
The origins of olive growing in Sardinia date to pre-Roman times. Spanish domination from the 14th to 18th centuries increased the number of varieties available and contributed new processing techniques.

SARDINIAN COOKING
Strangely enough, with just a few exceptions, traditional Sardinian cooking has more recipes for pork and kid than it does for seafood.

Pasta with Bottarga

Ingredients
- 1 lb/500 g spaghetti
- 2 cloves garlic, finely chopped
- 2 tbsp finely chopped parsley
- ¾ cup/200 ml extra-virgin olive oil
- 1¼ oz/40 g of freshly grated bottarga (dried mullet or tuna roe)
- freshly ground black pepper

Boil the spaghetti in a large pan of boiling, salted water until it is cooked *al dente*. Drain well and toss quickly in a large skillet (frying pan) with the garlic, parsley, and oil. Sprinkle with the bottarga, season, and serve.

Wine: a light, dry white (Alghero Vermentino)

Bottarga can be the roe of either mullet or tuna, although the mullet roe is considered to be of far higher quality. It is made by salting the fishes ovary sacs and then drying them in the sun. They are served with pasta, in salads, or thinly sliced on their own with a little extra-virgin olive oil.

FLAVOR
The bouquet of Sardinian oils almost all recall the scent of flowers. If export continues to grow as it has done in the last few years, they will soon be favorites on both Italian tables and abroad.

The seas of Sardinia remain crystal clear and inviting even today.

Index